IS THE ANTICHRIST ALIVE TODAY?

MARK HITCHCOCK

Multnomah®Publishers *Sisters, Oregon*

IS THE ANTICHRIST ALIVE TODAY?
published by Multnomah Publishers, Inc.

© 2002 by Mark Hitchcock

Cover design by Kirk DouPonce–UDG/DesignWorks
Cover images by Corbis

International Standard Book Number: 1-59052-075-0

Unless otherwise indicated, Scripture quotations are from:
New American Standard Bible® © 1960, 1977, 1995 by the Lockman
Foundation. Used by Permission.

Other Scripture quotations are from:
Holy Bible, New Living Translation (NLT) © 1996. Used by permission of
Tyndale House Publishers, Inc. All rights reserved.
The Holy Bible, King James Version (KJV)

Multnomah is a trademark of Multnomah Publishers, Inc.,
and is registered in the U.S. Patent and Trademark Office.
The colophon is a trademark of Multnomah Publishers, Inc.

Printed in the United States of America

For information:
MULTNOMAH PUBLISHERS, INC.
POST OFFICE BOX 1720
SISTERS, OREGON 97759

Library of Congress Cataloging-in-Publication Data
Hitchcock, Mark.
    Is the antichrist alive today? / by Mark Hitchcock.
        p. cm.
Includes bibliographical references.
    ISBN 1-59052-074-0 (pbk.)
    1. Antichrist. I. Title.
    BT985 .H58 2003
    236--dc21   2002011414
            03 04 05 06 07 08—10 9 8 7 6 5 4 3 2 1 0

DEDICATION

To Nathan and Glennda Hitchcock
and Larry and Elizabeth Awbrey.

Your love for me and our family is a source
of continued blessing and joy to my heart.
One of my greatest joys in life is
to see you faithfully leading your families by
example and word to follow our Lord.

Thank you for passing the torch
to the next generation in our family.

CONTENTS

INTRODUCTION

The term *Antichrist* immediately evokes a reaction within us. It's a word of mystery, evil, power, and fascination. There has probably never been a time in the last two thousand years when people were not curious about the Antichrist.

In a 1997 *U.S. News and World Report* poll, 49 percent of Americans said they believe there will be an Antichrist sometime in the future.[1] However, I've heard people question whether we should even think much about the Antichrist, let alone write or read an entire book about him. On the contrary, you might be surprised to know that there are more than one hundred passages of Scripture that describe the origin, nationality, character, career, kingdom, and final doom of the Antichrist.

Moreover, there is solid precedent in church history for thinking about the Antichrist.

- Irenaeus was bishop of Lyons in Gaul in the late second century A.D. In his work *Against Heresies* (5.30.1), Irenaeus discusses the Antichrist and his mark.
- Hippolytus, a disciple of Irenaeus, served as presbyter of Rome from about A.D. 200 to 235, when he died as a martyr. He wrote a treatise called *On Christ and Antichrist* in about A.D. 200. This is the first entire work devoted specifically to the Antichrist. Hippolytus gives many explicit details on the person and times of the Antichrist.
- Tertullian, the first major voice in Latin Christianity, also wrote about the Antichrist in one of his works entitled *Against Marcion* (5.3.24).
- The monk Adso, in A.D. 950, wrote a very interesting work titled *Letter on the Origin and Time of the Antichrist.*

The purpose of this book is to take a serious look at one of the most frequently asked questions in all of Bible prophecy—Is the Antichrist alive today?

I am asked this question on a fairly regular basis. Inquiring minds want to know. I was reading Billy Graham's daily question and answer column a while back in our local newspaper, and someone wrote in with this question: "I have heard about the person who will appear at the end of time, called the Antichrist, and I wonder if you think he is alive today?"[2]

With all that's going on in our world today, many people seem to have a sense that the time of the end could be very near and that Antichrist could appear soon.

However, before we can answer this specific question, we need to gain some background information and context concerning what the Bible says about the rise of Antichrist. Therefore, before we answer the big question we will spend a few chapters presenting some of the key activities of the Antichrist and seeing whether conditions in the world today seem to be ripe for his appearing.

Now, I know what you are tempted to do at this point. You want to jump right to the end to see the conclusion. But you must resist that temptation!

Reading the chapters in order will make the conclusion much more meaningful, because before we can answer the question we need to know who we are looking for.

What will he be like? Where will he come from? What events will pave the way for his coming? Is the world stage today set for his rise?

In this book, as with the others in this End Times Answers series, I am going to assume that the reader has at least a basic knowledge of a few key events in the end times. So to make sure you fully understand these events, let's begin with a brief review and define a few key terms that you will see sprinkled throughout the book.

THE RAPTURE OF THE CHURCH TO HEAVEN

This next event on God's prophetic timetable will occur when all who have personally trusted in Jesus Christ as their Savior, the living and the dead, will be caught up to meet the Lord in the air. They will go with Him back up to heaven, to return with Him to Earth at least seven years later at His second coming (see John 14:1–3; 1 Corinthians 15:50–58; 1 Thessalonians 4:13–18).

THE SEVEN-YEAR
TRIBULATION PERIOD

The tribulation is the final seven years of this age, which will begin with a peace treaty between Israel and Antichrist and will end with the second coming of Christ back to earth. During this time the Lord will pour out His wrath upon the earth in successive waves of judgment. But the Lord will also pour out His grace by saving millions of people during this time (see Revelation 6–19).

THE THREE-AND-A-HALF-YEAR
WORLD EMPIRE OF ANTICHRIST

In the last half of the Tribulation, Antichrist will rule the world politically, economically, and *religiously*. The entire world will give allegiance to him or suffer persecution and death (see Revelation 13:1–18).

THE CAMPAIGN OF ARMAGEDDON

The Campaign or War of Armageddon is the final event of the Great Tribulation, when all the armies of the earth gather to come against Israel and attempt once and for all to eradicate the Jewish people (see Revelation 14:19–20; 16:12–16; 19:19–21).

Introduction

THE SECOND COMING
OF CHRIST TO EARTH

The climactic event of human history is the literal, physical, visible, glorious return of Jesus Christ to planet earth to destroy the armies of the world gathered in Israel and to set up His kingdom on earth that will last for one thousand years (see Revelation 19:11–21).

God's Blueprint for the End Times

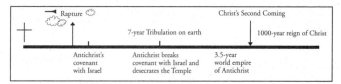

Amazingly, in a 1999 *Newsweek* poll 19 percent of Americans said they believe that the Antichrist is on earth now. That's one in five Americans who believes that the Antichrist is alive right now.

And in the same poll, nearly half of those who accept Biblical prophecy believe he is alive now.[3]

Could they be right?

Let's find out what the Bible has to say.

Maranatha!

"Our Lord, Come!"

Mark Hitchcock

THE COMING
WORLD RULER

Y ou might be as surprised as I was to learn that the three great world religions all contain prophecies of a towering, sinister world ruler in the end times. They are all looking for a man of unparalleled evil, an ultimate enemy, to emerge in the end times and take over the world.

In Islam, the person is called the Dajjal, which in Arabic means "deceiver." According to Islamic teaching, he will be a young man with one eye who will possess supernatural powers. He will be the incarnation of evil.

He will also claim to be God. He will gather seventy thousand Jewish followers, make a whirlwind tour of deception and destruction, set himself up as

ruler in Jerusalem, and finally be slain by Jesus at the Lydda Gate when Jesus returns from heaven. The Dajjal's emergence on the world scene is one of Islam's ten key signs of the end times.

Judaism teaches that a Roman ruler named Armilus will be a miracle worker who will lead his armies against Jerusalem. In the end, Armilus will be killed by Messiah ben David, or Messiah the Son of David, the true Messiah.

For Christians, the evil, end-time world ruler is known by many different names and titles. As A. W. Pink, the great theologian, notes, "Across the varied scenes depicted by prophecy there falls the shadow of a figure at once commanding and ominous. Under many different names, like the aliases of a criminal, his character and movements are set before us."[4]

Here are the top-ten aliases for the coming world ruler predicted in the Bible.

1. The little horn (see Daniel 7:8)
2. A king, insolent and skilled in intrigue (see Daniel 8:23)
3. The prince who is to come (see Daniel 9:26)
4. The one who makes desolate (see Daniel 9:27)

5. The king who does as he pleases (see Daniel 11:36)

6. A foolish shepherd (see Zechariah 11:15–17)

7. The man of lawlessness (see 2 Thessalonians 2:3)

8. The son of destruction (see 2 Thessalonians 2:3)

9. The rider on the white horse (see Revelation 6:2)

10. The Beast (see Revelation 13:1–9; 17:3, 8)

Without any doubt, the most commonly used and most familiar title in Christianity for the sinister end-time world ruler is *Antichrist*. Most people in America have heard this term and probably have at least some idea of what it means.

But to make doubly sure that we know who we are talking about, before we go any further let's pull over and park and define the word *Antichrist*.

"ANTI" CHRIST

The word *antichrist (antichristos)* is found only five times in the New Testament, all in the epistles of John (1 John 2:18, 22; 4:3; 2 John 7). In John's letters he is primarily concerned with the doctrinal error of denying the person of Jesus Christ. John states that even in his

own day many "antichrists" (false teachers) had arisen who were denying the true Christ and deceiving many (see 1 John 2:18).

The emphasis in John's epistles is on the immediate doctrinal error of his own day. However, the antichrists in John's day were only the initial "human embodiments" of the antichrist philosophy of Satan that was already working (1 John 4:3; 2 Thessalonians 2:7). John seems to look beyond his own day, and the many antichrists (small *a*), to the one supreme Antichrist (capital *A*) who will appear as the ultimate manifestation of the lawless system that denies Christ and deceives men.

1 John 2:18 says, "Children, it is the last hour; and just as you heard that antichrist is coming, even now many antichrists have appeared; from this we know that it is the last hour." John's readers knew about the predicted advent of the future, final Antichrist. They had heard that Antichrist was coming; in fact, John himself had probably taught them about the Antichrist, and they had certainly read about his coming in the Old Testament, in books such as Daniel. John's purpose was to warn his fellow

believers about present-day false teachers who came in the spirit of Antichrist, displaying hostility toward the true Christ.

The prefix *anti* can mean "against/opposed to" or "instead of/in place of." So the issue is, will the future Antichrist be "against" Christ or "in place of" Christ? That is, does *anti* mean "opposition" or "exchange"? Will he be a false, counterfeit Messiah, or will he simply "work against" Christ Himself?

Both of these meanings are undoubtedly included in the term *Antichrist.* He will be the archenemy and the ultimate opponent of the Lord Jesus. The origin, nature, and purpose of Christ and Antichrist are diametrically opposed. This list of titles reveals the gaping chasm between Christ and His adversary.[5]

CHRIST	ANTICHRIST
The Truth	The Lie
The Holy One	The Lawless One
The Man of Sorrows	The Man of Sin
The Son of God	The Son of Destruction
The Mystery of Godliness	The Mystery of Iniquity
The Lamb	The Beast

The total opposition of Antichrist to Christ is seen in these contrasting descriptions.[6]

FEATURE	CHRIST	ANTICHRIST
Origin	Heaven	Bottomless pit
Nature	The Good Shepherd	The foolish shepherd
Destiny	To be exalted on high	To be cast down into hell
Goal	To do His Father's will	To do his own will
Purpose	To save the lost	To destroy the holy people
Authority	His Father's name	His own name
Attitude	Humbled himself	Exalts himself
Fruit	The true vine	The vine of the earth
Response	Despised	Admired

In every area that can be imagined, Christ and Antichrist will be fundamentally opposed. But the Antichrist will also be "in place of" Christ. He will be an amazing parody or counterfeit of the true Christ. He will be a substitute Christ, a mock Christ, a pseudo Christ, an imitation Christ.

In John 5:43, Jesus said, "I have come in My Father's name, and you do not receive Me; if another

comes in his own name, you will receive him." The one coming in his own name will be the world's final false messiah, the Antichrist. He will attempt to be the "alter ego" of the true Christ.

As has often been pointed out, Satan has never originated anything except sin. He has always counterfeited the works of God. Antichrist is no exception. He is Satan's ultimate masterpiece—a false Christ and a forged replica of Jesus, the true Christ and Son of God.

Here are twenty ways that Antichrist will mimic the ministry of the true Son of God.

CHRIST	ANTICHRIST
Miracles, signs, and wonders (see Matthew 9:32–33; Mark 6:2)	Miracles, signs, and wonders (see Matthew 24:24; 2 Thessalonians 2:9)
Appears in the millennial temple (see Ezekiel 43:6–7)	Sits in the tribulation temple (see 2 Thessalonians 2:4)
Is God (see John 1:1–2; 10:36)	Claims to be God (see 2 Thessalonians 2:4)
Is the Lion from Judah (see Revelation 5:5)	Has a mouth like a lion (see Revelation 13:2)

CHRIST	ANTICHRIST
Makes a peace covenant with Israel (see Ezekiel 37:26)	Makes a peace covenant with Israel (see Daniel 9:27)
Causes men to worship God (see Revelation 1:6)	Causes men to worship Satan (see Revelation 13:3–4)
Followers sealed on their forehead (see Revelation 7:4; 14:1)	Followers sealed on their forehead or right hand (see Revelation 13:16–18)
Worthy name (see Revelation 19:16)	Blasphemous names (see Revelation 13:1)
Married to a virtuous bride (see Revelation 19:7–9)	Married to a vile prostitute (see Revelation 17:3–5)
Crowned with many crowns (see Revelation 19:12)	Crowned with ten crowns (see Revelation 13:1)
Is *the* King of kings- (see Revelation 19:16)	Is called "the king" (see Daniel 11:36)
Sits on a throne- (see Revelation 3:21; 12:5; 20:11)	Sits on a throne (see Revelation 13:2; 16:10)
Sharp sword from his mouth (see Revelation 19:15)	Bow in his hand (see Revelation 6:2)
Rides a white horse (see Revelation 19:11)	Rides a white horse (see Revelation 6:2)

CHRIST	ANTICHRIST
Has an army (see Revelation 19:14)	Has an army (see Revelation 19:19)
Violent death (see Revelation 5:6; 13:8)	Violent death (see Revelation 13:3)
Resurrection (see Matthew 28:6)	Resurrection (see Revelation 13:3, 14)
Second coming (see Revelation 19:11–21)	Second coming (see Revelation 17:8)
One-thousand-year worldwide kingdom (see Revelation 20:1–6)	Three-and-a-half-year worldwide kingdom (see Revelation 13:5–8)
Part of the Holy Trinity—Father, Son, and Holy Spirit (see 2 Corinthians 13:14)	Part of an unholy trinity—Satan, Antichrist, and False Prophet (see Revelation 13)

J. Dwight Pentecost aptly summarizes the meaning of the word *Antichrist.* "Satan is seeking to give the world a ruler in place of Christ who will also be in opposition to Christ so that he can rule over the world, instead of Christ."[7]

GETTING ACQUAINTED
WITH ANTICHRIST

There are three main places in the Bible that provide most of what we know about the coming world ruler: Daniel 7–12; 2 Thessalonians 2; and Revelation 13. Of these three passages, the one that sheds the most light on Antichrist is Revelation 13. In fact, we might call this the "Antichrist chapter" in the Bible.

Revelation 13:1–10 contains five key words that provide a quick, concise, yet comprehensive look at the Antichrist. All five of these words begin with the letter *w*.

Let's take a quick look at these five words as a summary of our introduction to the Antichrist.

1.   *Wound* (Revelation 13:3a, 12 ,14; 17:8)

Several passages in the book of Revelation clearly speak of the Antichrist's receiving a violent, fatal wound and then coming back to life.

> I saw one of his heads as if it had been slain, and his fatal wound was healed. Revelation 13:3a
> And he makes the earth and those who dwell

in it to worship the first beast, whose fatal wound was healed. Revelation 13:12
And he deceives…,telling those who dwell on the earth to make an image to the beast who had the wound of the sword and has come to life. Revelation 13:14
The beast that you saw was, and is not, and is about to come up out of the abyss and go to destruction. And those who dwell on the earth, whose name has not been written in the book of life from the foundation of the world, will wonder when they see the beast, that he was and is not and will come." Revelation 17:8

I believe this means that the Antichrist will be violently killed (probably assassinated) and will miraculously rise from the dead during the coming tribulation period. But any discussion of this issue always raises another question. Does Satan have the power to raise a dead person back to life?

Many maintain that he does not. They think that the Antichrist will only appear to die and will then fake a resurrection to deceive the world. However, the

words used to describe the "death" of the Antichrist are used in other places to describe a violent death. In Revelation 5:6, for instance, the same word is used of the death of Jesus Christ. Moreover, Revelation 17:8 says that, after the Antichrist is killed, he goes to the bottomless pit, or abyss, for a time before reappearing on earth. This doesn't seem to be describing someone who is faking his death.

I cannot explain every detail of how this death and resurrection will occur, but I believe that these passages lead us to a startling conclusion: God will permit Satan to perform this marvelous feat to advance his nefarious parody of Christ and further deceive the world.

For once, at least, Satan will have the power to raise someone from the dead.

2. *Wonder* (Revelation 13:3b; 17:8)

You can just imagine the overwhelming impact this event will have on the world. At the climax of history a great ruler will experience a healing that closely approximates the death and resurrection of Jesus Christ. Revelation 13:3–4 and 17:8 record the worldwide

amazement and wonder at the death and resurrection of the Antichrist.

> And all the world wondered after the beast. (Revelation 13:3b, KJV)
> The beast that you saw was, and is not, and is about to come up out of the abyss and go to destruction. And those who dwell on the earth, whose name has not been written in the book of life from the foundation of the world, will wonder when they see the beast, that he was and is not and will come. (Revelation 17:8)

This will be the greatest event in the history of the world as far as the people of earth are concerned. Imagine the assassination, the violent death, of the most charismatic, most effective politician the world has ever seen. The whole world will be in mourning. The collective angst will be profound.

It will be similar to the death of JFK in 1963 or of Lady Di in 1997. Everyone watches the funeral procession on television. Networks show nothing else. But suddenly, as the decorated hearse arrives at the ceme-

tery and the coffin is removed, the most incredible thing the world has ever seen transpires in front of the eyes of billions of people: The body rises up out of the coffin, the pallbearers recoil in terror and drop the casket, and the Antichrist walks calmly to the nearest microphone and begins to speak to a totally dumbfounded world.

One cannot even begin to imagine the scene. Can't you just picture the world news networks reporting this story! And the whole world will be filled with wonder.

3. *Worship* (Revelation 13:4, 8)

Wonder will quickly turn to worship. Satan will use this great event to exalt the Antichrist and himself to worldwide worship.

> They worshiped the dragon because he gave his authority to the beast; and they worshiped the beast, saying "Who is like the beast, and who is able to wage war with him?" (Revelation 13:4)
> All who dwell on the earth will worship him, everyone whose name has not been written

from the foundation of the world in the book of life of the Lamb who has been slain. (Revelation 13:8)

The Bible tells us in Revelation 17:8 that when the Antichrist is violently killed, he goes to the bottomless pit for a period of time and then comes back to life. During this brief time in the bottomless pit, he is completely energized by Satan. He probably receives his orders and strategy from Satan, literally selling his soul to the devil, and then comes back to earth with hellish ferocity to establish his dominion and worship over a completely awestruck world.

4.   *Words* (Revelation 13:5–6)

Antichrist will also be a man of great words. He will be a boaster, blasphemer, and braggart without peer. He will have a big mouth!

There was given to him a mouth speaking arrogant words and blasphemies, and authority to act for forty-two months was given to him. And he opened his mouth in blasphemies

against God, to blaspheme His name and His
tabernacle, that is, those who dwell in heaven.
Revelation 13:5–6

5. *War* (Revelation 13:7)

Last, but certainly not least, Antichrist will be a
man of war. He will rule the entire world for the final
forty-two months, or three and a half years, of this age.

> It was also given to him to make war with the
> saints and to overcome them, and authority
> over every tribe and people and tongue and
> nation was given to him. (Revelation 13:7)

CLUE

My wife, my sons, and I like to play a board game
called Clue. The game begins with the assumption
that someone has been murdered (a great theme for a
family game). The object of the game is to figure out,
by the process of elimination, who did it, where they
did it, and how they did it. When you get all the clues
you need, you solve the mystery.

We could call the next five chapters *Clue*. In these chapters we will look at five key clues from the Bible that should help us answer the question: Is the Antichrist alive today? We are going to look at five of the key Biblical prophecies concerning the Antichrist and at events in our world today to see how they match up.

Join me as we search for the clues that will help us determine if the stage is being set for his appearance.

THE LAST CAESAR

About 550 years before Christ, the Old Testament prophet Daniel had a great vision in which he saw four terrible beasts arising out of the sea: a lion with wings like an eagle, a lopsided bear with three ribs in his mouth, a leopard with four heads and four wings, and a terrible, strong, crushing beast with ten horns and large iron teeth (Daniel 7:1–7).

With the advantage of hindsight we know that these great beasts picture the four great world empires that ruled over Israel in succession from Daniel's day: Babylon (the lion), Medo-Persia (the bear), Greece (the leopard with four heads), and Rome (the beast with iron teeth).

But there is one problem. The fourth beast,

which represents Rome, has an unusual feature. It has ten horns, which Daniel says represent ten kings, or leaders, who rule simultaneously. These ten horns on this fourth beast correspond to the ten toes on the image in King Nebuchadnezzar's dream in Daniel 2.

The problem with this picture is that, according to history, the Roman Empire has never existed in a ten-kingdom form. It has never been ruled over by ten kings. Therefore, I believe this must be speaking of a final form of the Roman Empire that will be reunited in the end times and that will be ruling the world when Jesus returns.

When you think about it, unlike the other empires before it, the Roman Empire was never destroyed and replaced by another empire. It simply fell apart. But in the end times, the Bible teaches that it will be reunited or revived in a form that will be ruled by ten kings or powerful rulers.

I like to call this the unholy Roman Empire of the end times.

THE FIRST PROPHECY
OF ANTICHRIST

The first unmistakable prophecy of Antichrist in the Bible is found in Daniel 7:8. In this verse, the Antichrist is identified as a "little horn" who comes up among the ten horns who are ruling the last-days Roman Empire.

The first time someone or something is mentioned in the Bible is usually very important. The initial reference usually gives the key details that will be amplified later on. The first mention of Antichrist is no exception.

Daniel 7:8 says, "While I was contemplating the horns, behold, another horn, a little one, came up among them, and three of the first horns were pulled out by the roots before it; and behold, this horn possessed eyes like the eyes of a man and a mouth uttering great boasts."

This verse tells us four very important things about Antichrist that God doesn't want us to miss. It tells us *how* he will emerge on the world scene, *when* he will emerge, *where* he will emerge, and *what* he will do when he emerges.

First, he arises insignificantly in the beginning. He appears at first as a "little horn" among the ten horns. He will not come on the scene as a mighty power when he first appears.

Second, as we have already said, when he emerges on the world scene, the revived Roman Empire will exist in a ten-nation form. He is an eleventh horn that comes on the scene when the ten horns (kings or rulers) are in power.

Third, the Antichrist himself will rise up from within the reunited Roman Empire. Notice that Daniel 7:8 says the little horn "came up among them"; that is, among the ten horns who represent the final end-time form of the Roman Empire. In other words, he will be from the reunited Roman Empire.

His European, Roman nationality is confirmed in Daniel 9:26–27. These verses tell us that Antichrist will be of the same nationality as the people who destroyed the Jewish temple in A.D. 70, an event that was still future when Daniel wrote. With the benefit of hindsight we know that these people were the Romans. Therefore, it appears that the Antichrist will be of Roman origin.

Fourth, as he climbs to power, the Antichrist will destroy three of the kings in the reunited Roman Empire who apparently stand in his way. "And three of the first horns were pulled out by the roots before it" (Daniel 7:8).

THE EUROPEAN UNION

The European Union (EU) is hailed by many today as the reuniting, or reviving, of the Roman Empire. The EU today is often called EU-15 to indicate the number of nations that have joined: Austria, Belgium, Denmark, Finland, France, Germany, Greece, Ireland, Italy, Luxembourg, the Netherlands, Portugal, Spain, Sweden, and the United Kingdom.

The parliament of the EU has 626 members that serve five-year terms. There are also numerous councils, committees, and commissions that meet on a regular basis. The EU also rotates its presidency among the member nations every six months.

On January 1, 2002, the Euro became the official single currency of the EU. When the currency became official, a CNN report said, "For the first time since the Roman Empire, a large portion of Europe now

shares a common currency."[8] Twelve of the fifteen member states are now participating in the common currency—all but Great Britain, Sweden, and Denmark.

I believe this economic tie among the EU nations is significant. Now that they have a common currency, it is very difficult to see how they could revert back to their former currencies. This might be the glue that welds them together for good.

LITTLE BIG HORN

It's interesting to me that the ancient Roman Empire began as a republic with a democratically elected Senate and then regressed to rule by one man—Octavian, or Caesar Augustus. He was the first of a long line of men who ruled the Roman Empire as dictators.

I believe the same thing will happen in the reunited Roman Empire, or what we might call "Rome II." It has begun with a treaty-based institutional framework, and it manages economic and political cooperation among its fifteen member nations. It is represented by a 626-member parliament elected

directly by the people. However, the Bible indicates that the reunited Roman Empire will move to a dictatorship sometime after the Antichrist comes on the scene.

The little horn will uproot three of the ten kings and take control of the reunited Roman Empire (Daniel 7:8). He will do what Caesar Augustus did more than two thousand years ago; he will replace the republic with a ruler. One man to rule it all. Himself. In this way he will truly be the last Caesar.

It's not difficult to see how a man of great power, intellect, charisma, and will could someday rise to the presidency of the EU (which right now is a six-month rotating office). And then, when his six-month term is over, he will refuse to give it up. When a power struggle ensues, he overcomes the three leaders who try to block him. Then he takes over as the ten kings give him authority by consent (Revelation 17:12–13).

After he takes over the new Roman Empire, he sets his sights even higher. He takes steps to take over the entire world. And at the midpoint of the tribulation his dream becomes a nightmarish reality.

EU-10?

Currently, there are fifteen nations in the EU, not ten as the Bible predicts will be present in the reunited Roman Empire of the end times. Therefore, we must say that the present state of the EU *is not* the reunited Roman Empire in the ten-kingdom or ten-king form predicted in Daniel 2, Daniel 7, Revelation 13, and Revelation 17.

But what I'm suggesting is that we can see movements in Europe today that are preparing the way for the advent of the little horn, or Antichrist, as predicted in Scripture. It doesn't take a very active imagination to see how the ten-king form the Bible predicts could gel out of the current situation in Europe.

COINCIDENCE OR CONVERGENCE?

Interestingly, the movie *The Omen* begins with the birth of the Antichrist in a dimly lit hospital in Rome. A chilling poem from this same movie reinforces the belief that the coming Antichrist will arise from the reunited Roman Empire.

When the Jews return to Zion,
    And a comet rips the sky,
And the Holy Roman Empire rises,
    Then you and I must die.
From the eternal sea he rises,
    Creating armies on either shore,
Turning man against his brother,
    'Til man exists no more.

As we look at our world today, the Jews are returning to Zion. Several passages of Scripture predict that the Jews must be regathered to their land in the end times for the final events of this age to come to pass (see Daniel 9:27; Ezekiel 37:11–12; 38:8). They are in the process of being regathered to their land after a two-thousand-year absence. Modern Israel became a nation on May 14, 1948.

And the *unholy* Roman Empire, 1,600 years after its breakup, seems to be coming back together in the European Union. Most people track the beginning of the EU back to the Treaty of Rome in 1957, when six European nations joined together in a loose economic alliance.

Could these incredible events that happened within ten years of each other, and that continue to gain momentum today, be coincidences? I don't think so. They are both described in the Bible as key signs of the end times.

What we see today could very well be setting the stage for these events the Bible predicts. It appears to me that events that are necessary to prepare the world for the final drama of the ages are converging right before our eyes.

The rise of Antichrist may not be far behind!

THE PEACEMAKER

I t is a riddle wrapped up in a mystery inside an
enigma."

In a speech broadcast October 1, 1939, that's how
Sir Winston Churchill described the actions of the
Russians in his day. But what he said about Russian
actions could be applied to the Middle East today.

Let me ask you a very simple question. What is the
number one international political problem today that
the world would love to see resolved? That's easy isn't it?

Israel.

The Palestinian-Israeli problem is an unsolvable
mess for the world's greatest diplomats. "It is a riddle
wrapped up in a mystery inside an enigma."

But did you know that when Antichrist comes on
the scene, that will all change—temporarily? His official

introduction to the world will be a great gesture of peace that will solve the Middle East peace problem.

THE MIDDLE EAST
PEACE ACCORD

Antichrist will first appear to be a great peacemaker. Daniel 9:27 says that the event that begins the seven-year tribulation period is the signing of a covenant between Antichrist and Israel. "And he [the Antichrist] will make a firm covenant with the many for one week [one week of years, or seven years], but in the middle of the week he will put a stop to sacrifice and grain offering."

It seems that the covenant Antichrist makes with Israel may be an imposed peace. Daniel describes it as a "firm covenant." The word *firm* in Hebrew carries the idea of a "strong, forced, or compelled covenant."[9]

As the head of a powerful, multinational confederation, he will have the power and skill to initiate, formulate, and impose a peace covenant on Israel and possibly her neighbors.

Concerning the nature of this peace treaty, prophecy scholar John Walvoord says,

When a Gentile ruler over the ten nations imposes a peace treaty on Israel, it will be from superior strength and will not be a negotiated peace treaty, but it apparently will include the necessary elements for such a contract. It will include the fixing of Israel's borders, the establishment of trade relations with her neighbors—something she does not enjoy at the present time, and, most of all, it will provide protection from outside attacks, which will allow Israel to relax her military preparedness. It can also be anticipated that some attempts will be made to open the holy areas of Jerusalem to all faiths related to it.[10]

The idea of an imposed peace on Israel by a confederation of Western nations seems like a very probable scenario today. One can easily see in today's environment how Antichrist could come on the scene and give Israel an imposed peace. A take it or leave it deal.

As the world grows more frustrated with the situation in the Middle East, many are running low on patience. An imposed, forced peace by the leader of

the Western world could certainly be a possible scenario in light of current events in the Middle East.

One important part of this covenant will be to give the Jewish people renewed access to the Temple Mount, to offer sacrifices in a rebuilt temple. For the Antichrist to put a stop to Jewish sacrifices at the midpoint of the Tribulation, as Daniel 9:27 says, the sacrificial system must have been previously instituted.

However, whatever the exact nature of this covenant is, the result is peace and security for Israel.

This same period of peace is mentioned by the prophet Ezekiel, where Israel is described in the latter years as living in unsuspecting peace, safety, tranquility, and prosperity (see Ezekiel 38:8, 11, 14).

PEACE AND SAFETY

The New Testament also speaks of this brief time of peace at the beginning of the tribulation period before the terrible wrath of God is unleashed. "For you yourselves know full well that the day of the Lord will come just like a thief in the night. While they are saying, 'Peace and safety!' then destruction will come upon them suddenly like labor pains upon a woman

with child, and they will not escape" (1 Thessalonians 5:2–3).

THE RIDER ON
THE WHITE HORSE

Revelation 6:1–2, which is the beginning of John's vision of the seven-year tribulation period, describes the Antichrist and his overtures of peace under the symbolism of a rider on a white horse.[11] "Then I saw when the Lamb broke one of the seven seals, and I heard one of the four living creatures saying as with a voice of thunder, 'Come.' I looked, and behold, a white horse, and he who sat on it had a bow; and a crown was given to him, and he went out conquering and to conquer" (Revelation 6:1–2).

Notice the Antichrist rides a white horse to imitate the true Christ (see Revelation 19:11), and he carries a bow but no arrows. This suggests that at first his conquest is a diplomatic, bloodless one. He will threaten war but achieve his victory through peace. He will conceal his iron fist in the velvet glove of "peace."

This interpretation is confirmed by the fact that the next rider is a rider on a red horse, which pictures

war and slaughter. The rider on the red horse carries "a great sword" and will "take peace from the earth" (Revelation 6:4).

Obviously, if peace is removed from the earth by the rider on the second horse, then peace must be present before it can be removed. That peace is the imposed peace of Antichrist, the rider on the white horse.

For his efforts, Antichrist will undoubtedly win the Nobel Peace Prize and be hailed as *Time*'s Man of the Year.

"PEACE, PEACE!"

The world today is crying for peace, especially in the Middle East. And Israel is in the world spotlight. This is exactly what we should expect as we look at God's blueprint of the end times.

I can't help but imagine that the ceremony for Antichrist's covenant of peace will be something like the peace accord signed on the White House lawn between Yitzhak Rabin and Yasser Arafat in 1993. All the world's great leaders will be present. The atmosphere will be filled with pomp and pageantry. The

world will have finally achieved its goal. "Peace" will finally be in man's grasp.

The world today is ready for the rider on the white horse!

He may be getting ready to mount up very soon.

ANTICHRIST IN THE TEMPLE OF GOD

L ocation, location, location."

As most buyers and sellers know, these are the three most important words in real estate. The same can be said when it comes to God's plan for the end times. Location is everything.

According to the prophetic Scriptures, the most important piece of real estate on earth is the tiny land of Israel. No bigger than the size of New Jersey, it is the focal point of the key events of Bible prophecy.

But to narrow it down even further, within Israel the most important location is the capital city of Jerusalem. And within Jerusalem, the most important location is the thirty-five-acre area known as the Temple Mount.

THE THIRD TEMPLE

God's Word mentions four Jewish temples that have stood or will stand in the future on this sacred site known as the Temple Mount.

1. The temple of Solomon—Constructed in 960 B.C. by Solomon; destroyed in 586 B.C. by the Babylonians
2. The temple of Zerubbabel and Herod— Originally constructed by Zerubbabel in 538–515 B.C.; embellished and expanded by Herod the Great beginning in 19 B.C.; destroyed by the Romans in A.D. 70
3. The tribulation temple—Future
4. The millennial temple—Future

The Bible predicts that, in the end times, the Jewish people will build another temple, a third one, on the site of the Temple Mount in Jerusalem. This temple is often referred to as the tribulation temple.

Five key passages in the Bible speak of a specific action taken by the Antichrist in the middle of the Tribulation, in relation to this tribulation temple.

1. *Daniel 9:27* "And he will make a firm covenant with the many for one week, but in the middle of the week he will put a stop to sacrifice and grain offering; and on the wing of abominations will come one who makes desolate, even until a complete destruction, one that is decreed, is poured out on the one who makes desolate."

2. *Daniel 12:11* "From the time that the regular sacrifice is abolished and the abomination of desolation is set up, there will be 1,290 days."

3. *Matthew 24:15* "Therefore when you see the ABOMINATION OF DESOLATION which was spoken of through Daniel the prophet, standing in the holy place...."

4. *2 Thessalonians 2:4* "...who opposes and exalts himself above every so-called god or object of worship, so that he takes his seat in the temple of God, displaying himself as being God." (In other words, the Antichrist will sit in the rebuilt temple in Jerusalem during the Tribulation, proclaiming himself to be God.

5. *Revelation 11:1–2* "Then there was given me a

measuring rod like a staff; and someone said, 'Get up and measure the temple of God and the altar, and those who worship in it. Leave out the court which is outside the temple and do not measure it, for it has been given to the nations; and they will tread under foot the holy city for forty-two months.'"

These passages make it abundantly clear that the Jewish people will rebuild the temple in Jerusalem sometime before the midpoint of the coming tribulation period.

THE ABOMINATION
OF DESOLATION

For at least some of the time during the first half of the Tribulation, the Jewish people, under their covenant with Antichrist, will offer sacrifices in the rebuilt temple (see Daniel 9:27).

However, at the midpoint of the seven-year tribulation period, that will all change. Daniel 9:27b says, "but in the middle of the week he will put a stop to sacrifice and grain offering; and on the wing of abominations

will come one who makes desolate, even until a complete destruction, one that is decreed, is poured out on the one who makes desolate."

At this point, the Antichrist will break his covenant with Israel and commit an act that is most often called "the abomination of desolation."

What exactly is the abomination of desolation? First, the word *abomination* refers to an idol or an image. Second, the first reference to the abomination of desolation in Daniel 9:27 links it with Antichrist's breaking of the covenant with Israel and the temple. The phrase "on the wing of abominations" refers to the pinnacle of the temple, emphasizing the idea of an overspreading influence. In other words, what begins at the temple will spread to other places.[12] The abomination of desolation, then, is an idol or image that desolates the temple and spreads out from there to the world.

There are probably two main elements, or phases, involved in the abomination of desolation. The first element is described for us in 2 Thessalonians 2:3–4:

> Let no one in any way deceive you, for it will
> not come unless the apostasy comes first, and

the man of lawlessness is revealed, the son of
destruction, who opposes and exalts himself
above every so-called god or object of worship,
so that he takes his seat in the temple of God,
displaying himself as being God.

In his initial takeover of Jerusalem, Antichrist will
sit in the place of God in the very Holy of Holies in
the temple, declaring to the world that he is God and
thus establishing the final false religion that he will
impose on the entire world.

The second aspect of the abomination of desolation is described in Revelation 13:11–15.

Then I saw another beast coming up out of
the earth; and he had two horns like a lamb
and he spoke as a dragon. He exercises all the
authority of the first beast in his presence. And
he makes the earth and those who dwell in it
to worship the first beast, whose fatal wound
was healed. He performs great signs, so that he
even makes fire come down out of heaven to
the earth in the presence of men. And he

deceives those who dwell on the earth because of the signs which it was given him to perform in the presence of the beast, telling those who dwell on the earth to make an image to the beast who had the wound of the sword and has come to life. And it was given to him to give breath to the image of the beast, so that the image of the beast would even speak and cause as many as do not worship the image of the beast to be killed.

The Antichrist's right-hand man, who is called the false prophet, will be given the authority to do great signs and wonders, deceiving people into worshiping the beast. His greatest deception will be the construction of an image, or likeness, of the Antichrist that will speak.

This image will be placed in the Holy of Holies in the temple in Jerusalem to carry forward the abomination of desolation. Jerusalem will serve as the Antichrist's religious capital, and the temple will serve as the center of worship with the living image standing in its inner precinct. In this way, Satan will

counterfeit God's presence in the Holy of Holies in Solomon's temple. All the earth will be required to worship the beast and his image or to face death.

The two phases of the abomination of desolation, therefore, will be the declaration of the deity of the Antichrist in the Holy of Holies in the temple at the midpoint of the tribulation, followed by the setting up of his image in the same place. This condition will go on for the final 1,260 days, or three and a half years, of the tribulation period.[13]

BETWEEN THE ROCK AND A HARD PLACE

The main impediment to the rebuilding of a temple in Jerusalem is the presence of the Muslim Dome of the Rock, or the Mosque of Omar, on the place where the temple must be rebuilt. Also on the Temple Mount is the Al-Aqsa Mosque, which was completed in A.D. 715 and which is regarded as the third holiest place in Islam (after Mecca and Medina). However, Muslims consider the Dome of the Rock to be the crown of the Temple Mount.

How will the Jews ever be able to rebuild their

temple, with the Dome of the Rock on the same piece of real estate, without triggering World War III? To me this is one of the thorniest problems in all of Bible prophecy.

However, there are several possible solutions that are commonly put forth.[14] I believe that the simplest one is for the Antichrist, when he comes to power, to impose a peace treaty on Israel and the Islamic/Arab nations. A key element in that plan would have to include Israeli sovereignty over the Temple Mount area. The Antichrist will then do what no one has been able to do up to that point. He will bring a comprehensive peace plan to the Middle East. If he is able to somehow compel Muslims to give up control of the Temple Mount and return it to the Jews, he certainly would be hailed as the greatest diplomat in human history. This may be the event that catapults him onto the international political scene as the world's messiah.

READY TO REBUILD?

We have to admit that the Bible doesn't tell us specifically how the temple will be rebuilt. We don't know what conditions will come about to make the temple

a reality. But one thing is sure—the temple will be rebuilt in Jerusalem just as God's Word predicts! And there are some amazing preparations going on in Jerusalem today among the Jewish people for the rebuilding of the third Jewish temple.

The Temple Institute in Jerusalem is vigorously working to construct needed objects and utensils for renewed worship in the third temple, including the menorah of pure gold, the pure gold crown worn by the high priest, firepans and shovels, the mitzraq (vessel used to transport the blood of sacrificial offerings), the copper laver, linen garments of the priests, stone vessels to store the ashes of the red heifer, and so on. There are ongoing efforts to produce an unblemished red heifer to fulfill the purification requirements of Numbers 19:1–10.

Randall Price, the foremost evangelical authority on the temple, concludes his excellent, up-to-date book on the temple with these words.

What does this say to you and me? It says that not only have the Jews already begun the ascent to their goal, but they are only one step

away from accomplishing it! As this book has shown, the current conflict over the Temple Mount and the resolve of the Jewish activists to prepare for the conclusion of this conflict have provided the momentum for the short distance that remains of the climb. We live in a day that is on the brink of the rebuilding effort, and with it the beginning of the fulfillment of the prophecies that will move the world rapidly to see as a reality the coming Last Days Temple.[15]

Two of the key things that had to happen for the temple to be rebuilt have already occurred. First, the Jews are back in their land, and they have control of Jerusalem. All that remains is for them to have sovereignty over the Temple Mount.

When they get it, the temple will be rebuilt, and Antichrist's desolation of it won't be far behind.

The events we see today are paving the way for prophecy to be fulfilled.

ONE WORLD UNDER ANTICHRIST

A few years ago I fulfilled my parental duty and took my family on our pilgrimage to the modern American Mecca. Of course, I'm talking about the required family trek to Disney World and Universal Studios in Orlando. As much as I dreaded the crowds, I have to admit I had a great time.

My boys and I loved the roller coasters. The bigger, the better. Our favorites were Space Mountain and Dueling Dragons (which I never ended up riding, by the way). But my wife's favorite ride was a peaceful, beautiful ride called It's a Small World. The main thing I remember about the ride is that the song that plays throughout the whole ride is the Disney favorite—"It's a Small World."

I don't know what the original author of this song had in mind when it was written, but it could certainly be the theme song of our world today.

Globalism and *globalization* are the watchwords of our times. The world is getting smaller every day. The decade of the 1990s has been called the "decade of globalization."

"HONEY, I SHRUNK THE WORLD"

I'll never forget doing my laundry back before I got married. I would do the wash and then hang up all my cotton polo shirts to drip-dry so they wouldn't shrink in the dryer. Well, you guessed it. One time, as I threw the other clothes in the dryer, I accidentally put one of my extra large 100 percent–cotton polo shirts in the hot dryer. And of course, it was my favorite shirt. When I pulled it out forty-five minutes later, it was a small at best. It would have fit a young boy.

The shrinkage was fast, drastic, and permanent.

That's exactly what I have seen happen to the world in my lifetime. When I was born in 1959, the world was still an extra large place divided neatly into

its various parts. But today it's small. Very small. And it all happened so quickly. The world has shrunk before our eyes, and the process continues at lightning speed. We have gone from tribalism to nationalism to globalism. Who would have dreamed, forty or fifty years ago, that the world would be what it is today?

Numerous factors have contributed to world shrinkage.

- The end of the cold war (the world is no longer divided into two major blocs of nations)
- The speed of travel from one continent to another (leaders and armies can travel thousands of miles at lightning speed)
- Incredible advances in communications (world news programs, computers, the Internet, and satellites bring instant communication)
- Modern weapons of mass destruction (some form of world government seems to be the only human solution for a world that can destroy itself)
- Modern surveillance technology (makes it possible to know where people, troops, and

weapons are, and what they are doing)

- The intertwining of world markets, currencies, stock markets, and economies (makes it easy to invest in, or to divest from, any market, using any currency anywhere in the world)
- Terrorism and the rise of rogue states (apart from God, globalism and a world government is the only sensible path available to man to contain rogue states and terrorism)
- Global problems such as starvation, pollution, and climatic instability (these problems show that the world can be saved only through international cooperation)

Indeed, the world is shrinking before our eyes. Many leaders today maintain that man's only hope for survival is some form of world government. And I don't believe this state of affairs is an accident.

THE MAN WHO WOULD BE GOD

Globalism and the movement toward world government strikingly foreshadow the picture of the end times presented in Scripture. The Bible reveals that the

final three and a half years of this age will be dominated by Antichrist as he rules the entire world politically, economically, and religiously (see Revelation 13:1–18). The entire world will be under the thumb of his complete domination:

Antichrist will rule the world politically—"And authority over every tribe and people and tongue and nation was given to him" (Revelation 13:7b).

Antichrist will rule the world economically—"And he provides that no one will be able to buy or to sell, except the one who has the mark, either the name of the beast or the number of his name" (Revelation 13:17).

Antichrist will rule the world religiously—"All who dwell on the earth will worship him" (Revelation 13:8a).

When you think about it, even as recently as thirty years ago it would have been virtually impossible to rule the entire world in the manner that the Bible predicts.

But now that's all changed. The necessary ingredients for a world government and world ruler are present today for the first time in human history.

ONE MORE CLUE

I believe all of this is happening according to God's sovereign plan for this world. God's prophetic plan is right on schedule. And globalism is another piece of the prophetic puzzle that is preparing the way for the Antichrist.

It's just one more clue that the rise of Antichrist may not be far away.

A MAN WHO
MAKES HIS MARK

The church I have the privilege of pastoring is Faith Bible Church in Edmond, Oklahoma. When we were first establishing our street address at our current site, the postal service told us we could choose any number from 500 to 699 North Coltrane. One man in our church suggested that we select the address 666 North Coltrane, since it would certainly get people's attention and be easy to remember. I have to admit that since I love Bible prophecy so much, this suggestion almost tempted me above what I was able to bear. However, my better judgment finally took over, and we settled for the more mundane 600 North Coltrane.

The number 666, the so-called mark of the beast,

may be one of the most intriguing issues in all of Bible prophecy. There has probably been more speculation, sensationalism, and just plain silliness about this issue than any other I can think of in Bible prophecy.

Let's consider what Scripture really says about the mark of the beast.

6 6 6

In the movie *The Omen*, Damien was born on June 6, at 6:00 (666) to symbolize his identification as the coming Antichrist. Almost everyone, including the most biblically illiterate people, have heard something about 666, or the mark of the beast.

Revelation 13:16–18 is the key passage on the meaning of 666, or the mark of the beast.

> And he causes all, the small and the great, and the rich and the poor, and the free men and the slaves, to be given a mark on their right hand or on their forehead, and he provides that no one will be able to buy or to sell, except the one who has the mark, either the name of the beast or the number of his name.

Here is wisdom. Let him who has understanding calculate the number of the beast, for the
number is that of a man; and his number is six
hundred and sixty-six.

As you can imagine, there are several explanations
of what 666 means. But I believe the best one is the use
of a process called gematria. In gematria, a numerical
value is attributed to each of the letters of the alphabet.
If you want to find the numerical total of a word or
name, you add together the values of each of its letters.

Hebrew, Latin, Greek, and English all have
numerical values for each letter in the alphabet. For
the Hebrew language, each letter in the twenty-two
letter Hebrew alphabet is assigned a numerical value as
follows: 1, 2, 3, 4, 5, 6, 7, 8, 9, 10, 20, 30, 40, 50, 60,
70, 80, 90, 100, 200, 300, and 400.

Revelation 13:16–18 provides five key clues that
aid in the interpretation of the mark of the beast. I
believe they support the idea that gematria is involved.
Read Revelation 13:16–18 again and notice the progression of the phrases.

1. The name of the beast
2. The number representing his name
3. The number of the beast
4. The number of a man
5. The number is 666[16]

When these five clues are followed through their logical progression, the number or mark of the beast is the number of a man who is the Antichrist or final world ruler. This number is the number of the Antichrist's own name.

As prophecy scholar Arnold Fruchtenbaum notes,

In this passage, whatever the personal name of the Antichrist will be, if his name is spelled out in Hebrew characters, the numerical value of his name will be 666. So this is the number that will be put on the worshipers of the Antichrist. Since a number of different calculations can equal 666, it is impossible to figure the name out in advance. But when he does appear, whatever his personal name will be, it will equal 666. Those who are wise (verse 18)

at that time will be able to point him out in advance.[17]

When the Antichrist begins to appear on the world scene at the beginning of the Tribulation, those who have understanding of God's Word will be able to identify him by the number of his name. The numerical value of his name will be 666.

Many have grossly misused gematria to apply it to the names of modern leaders to see if they could be the Antichrist. It has been applied to Henry Kissinger and Lyndon Johnson, and I have been told that both of their names equal 666. It has also been successfully tried out on JFK, Gorbachev, and Ronald Reagan. Supposedly *Bill Gates III* equals 666. *MS-DOS 6.21* equals 666 as does *Windows 95* and *System 7.0*.

I received a call from a man recently who told me emphatically that Philip Borbon Carlos, son of Juan Carlos of Spain, is the Antichrist because each of his three names contains six letters.

All such foolish speculation should be avoided. The Antichrist will not be unveiled until the beginning of the tribulation period, or Day of the Lord (see

2 Thessalonians 2:2–3). At that time people will be able to identify him because the number of his name will be 666.

"Here is wisdom. Let him who has understanding calculate the number of the beast, for the number is that of a man; and his number is six hundred and sixty six" (Revelation 13:18).

666 VERSUS 888

One might ask why the Lord planned for Antichrist's name to equal 666. Many prophecy teachers have pointed out that the triple six refers to man's number, which is the number six, one short of God's perfect number, seven. Remember, man was created on the sixth day.

Prophecy scholar John Walvoord writes,

Though there may be more light cast on it at the time this prophecy is fulfilled, the passage itself declares that this number is man's number. In the book of Revelation, the number seven is one of the most significant numbers indicating perfection. Accordingly, there are

seven seals, seven trumpets, seven bowls of the wrath of God, seven thunders, etc. This beast claims to be God, and if that were the case, he should be 777. This passage, in effect, says, No, you are only 666. You are short of deity even though you were originally created in the image and likeness of God. Most of the speculation on the meaning of this number is without profit or theological significance.[18]

M. R. DeHaan, the founder of the Radio Bible Class, also held this position.

Six is the number of man. Three is the number of divinity. Here is the interpretation. The beast will be a man who claims to be God. Three sixes imply that he is a false god and a deceiver, but he is nevertheless merely a man, regardless of his claims. Seven is the number of divine perfection, and 666 is one numeral short of seven. This man of sin will reach the highest peak of power and wisdom, but he will still be merely a man.[19]

It is interesting to me that the number of the name *Jesus* in Greek is 888, and each of his eight names in the New Testament (Lord, Jesus, Christ, Lord Jesus, Jesus Christ, Christ Jesus, Lord Christ, and Lord Jesus Christ) all have numerical values that are multiples of eight. I don't believe this is a coincidence. Jesus is complete perfection, while man, apart from God, is complete failure.

Jesus is the true God who proved His deity by being raised on Sunday, the "eighth day" of the week.[20]

WILL THAT BE THE RIGHT HAND OR THE FOREHEAD?

When the Beast, or Antichrist, seizes power at the middle of the Tribulation, all people on earth will be faced with a monumental decision. Will they take the mark of the beast on their right hand or forehead, or will they refuse the mark and face death? Will they take the mark that is required for every private and public transaction, or will they stand firm and say no to Antichrist?

The word *mark* in Greek *(charagma)* means "a

brand" or "tattoo" and signifies ownership, loyalty or protection.

As Henry Morris observes,

> The nature of the mark is not described, but the basic principle has been established for years in various nations. The social security card, the draft registration card, the practice of stenciling an inked design on the back of the hand, and various other devices are all fore-runners of this universal branding. The word itself ("mark") is the Greek *charagma*. It is used only in Revelation, to refer to the mark of the beast (eight times), plus one time to refer to idols 'graven by art and man's device' (Acts 17:29). The mark is something like an etching or a tattoo which, once inscribed, cannot be removed, providing a permanent (possibly eternal) identification as a follower of the Beast and the dragon.[21]

The issue for each person alive during the Tribulation will be, will I swear allegiance to this man

who claims to be God? Will I give up ownership of my life to him by taking his mark, or will I bow my knee to the true God only, lose my right to buy and sell, and even face beheading? (see Revelation 20:4).

The Antichrist's economic policy will be very simple: Take my mark and worship me, or starve. But it will be far better to refuse Antichrist and starve or face beheading, because by receiving his mark a person will forfeit eternal life. All who take the mark of the beast will face the eternal judgment of God. Taking the mark will seal their everlasting doom.

Revelation 14:9–10 says,

Then another angel, a third one, followed them, saying with a loud voice, "If anyone worships the beast and his image, and receives a mark on his forehead or on his hand, he also will drink of the wine of the wrath of God, which is mixed in full strength in the cup of His anger; and he will be tormented with fire and brimstone in the presence of the holy angels and in the presence of the Lamb. And the smoke of their torment goes up forever

and ever; they have no rest day and night, those who worship the beast and his image, and whoever receives the mark of his name."

"On Your Mark..."

The Antichrist's mark is significant for at least two reasons. First, his ability to force the whole world to take his mark signifies his worldwide power and authority. Think of the raw power that it will take to make everyone on the earth receive this mark or be killed.

Second, the mark allows the Antichrist to get an even stronger stranglehold on the world population. By means of this mark he will control the life of every person on earth. John Walvoord writes: "There is no doubt that with today's technology, a world ruler, who is in total control, would have the ability to keep a continually updated census of all living persons and know day by day precisely which people had pledged their allegiance to him and received the mark and which had not."[22]

But what will this mark be? Will it be something as simple as a tattoo? Will it be some kind of ID card?

Will it be a chip placed under the skin? The text of Revelation 13:16 strongly implies that the mark will be placed "on" or "upon" the hand or forehead, that is, on the outside where it can be seen. It seems to be something visible that must be shown to carry out any business or commercial transaction.

There has been all kind of unwarranted speculation on the exact nature of the mark of the beast. As my friend Dr. Harold Willmington says, "There's been a lot of sick, sick, sick about six, six, six."

The truth is, we really don't know, and we shouldn't waste a lot of time thinking about it. But what we can safely and responsibly say is that the technology is certainly available today to tattoo, brand, or partially embed an identifying number or mark on the skin of every person alive, to regulate world commerce and control people's lives.

TECHNOLOGY TODAY

I was amazed on Friday, May 10, 2002, to turn on NBC's *Today Show* and see the Jacobs family of Florida become media spectacles. They were the first family in America to have the new VeriChip implanted.

Every major media outlet in America was there. The whole process was presented as helpful, painless, simple, and…normal. The small chip, about the size of a grain of rice, was inserted into the upper arm with a needle.

The chip can contain one's entire medical history and can be tied in with the Global Positioning System so that any person with the chip can be located within minutes anywhere on earth.

We can all see how this will be very appealing. Think of all the time it will save at the doctor's office or emergency room. Think of how much better it would make you feel if your children had this chip and one of them got lost or was abducted.

Someone suggested you could even have the chip placed in your dog so you could find him when he digs out of the yard or forgets to come home for dinner.

But chip technology isn't the only thing out there. Many today are pointing out that, as the world becomes a more dangerous place, people are going to be forced to choose between privacy and security. In the aftermath of September 11, many have called for

some form of national ID card, biometric identification (thumbprint or eye scan), or some other form of digitizing or scanner technology not even invented yet.[23]

MISSING THE MARK

Again, let me make it clear, I'm not saying that any of these are the mark-of-the-beast technology. In many ways, any of these new technologies could prove very helpful in saving lives. Nothing that we see today is the mark of the beast. We don't know what method Antichrist will adopt to make his mark.

The only point I'm making is that today there is incredible technology available for the Antichrist to employ when he comes on the scene. He'll be able to control the life of every person on earth by a simple "mark" on the right hand or forehead. And this technology will inevitably become so commonplace in the years ahead that people will readily accept it without any hesitation or reservation. Ironically, to many people it will probably make more and more sense to use such advances in technology for "protection" in an increasingly dangerous world.

What specific method will Antichrist use? We don't know. But the rise of these amazing new means of locating, identifying, and controlling people's lives foreshadows the scenario depicted in Revelation 13.

It's just another clue that points to the picture Scripture paints of the end times.

WILL THE REAL ANTICHRIST PLEASE STAND UP?

Now that we have all the clues before us, you might be waiting for me to identify the Antichrist. But not so fast. There's one more important point we need to understand.

The Bible says that a key event must occur before the world can know the identity of the Antichrist.

That event is the Rapture!

Let's see how the Rapture fits into God's blueprint of the end times, especially in relation to the unveiling of the Antichrist.

FIRST THE RAPTURE!

T he identity of Antichrist has intrigued people for two thousand years. Many have found the temptation to identify the Antichrist irresistible. There have been numerous candidates, including Emperor Frederick II, Pope Innocent IV, Muhammad, the Turks, Napoleon, Hitler, Mussolini, Stalin, Mikhail Gorbachev (who some said had the mark of the beast on his forehead), Bill Clinton, or whomever the person making the claim happens to dislike.

As alluring as it may be at times to point someone out as the man of sin, we must avoid this temptation. Those who do so in spite of all warnings often draw a great deal of attention for a while, but they highlight the danger of trying to specifically identify the

Antichrist before the proper time.

A key Scripture passage in the New Testament, 2 Thessalonians 2:1–8, teaches us that the Rapture must come before the revelation of Antichrist. In other words, believers cannot know who the Antichrist is before we are raptured to heaven.

Let's look briefly at 2 Thessalonians 2:1–8 and see what it teaches us about the relationship between the Rapture and the appearance of Antichrist.

THE DAY OF THE LORD

In 2 Thessalonians, Paul is writing the Thessalonian believers to clear up some confusion they had about the coming Day of the Lord (which I believe begins with the seven-year tribulation period). Evidently, someone had taught them that they were already in the Tribulation. Paul corrects this error by pointing out that the Day of the Lord can't come until two things happen: (1) a great apostasy, or rebellion, and (2) the revelation of the Antichrist, or man of lawlessness.

Second Thessalonians 2:1–3 says,

Now we request you, brethren, with regard to the coming of our Lord Jesus Christ and our gathering together to Him, that you not be quickly shaken from your composure or be disturbed either by a spirit or a message or a letter as if from us, to the effect that the day of the Lord has come. Let no one in any way deceive you, for it will not come unless the apostasy comes first, and the man of lawlessness is revealed, the son of destruction.

Since, as I believe, the Antichrist will be revealed at the beginning of the Day of the Lord (the tribulation period) and the church will be raptured before this time, it doesn't appear that Christians will know the identity of the Antichrist before we are taken to heaven.

If you ever do figure out who the Antichrist is, then I've got bad news for you—you've been left behind!

Sometime after the Rapture, Antichrist will come on the scene to sign his peace covenant with Israel, and then the Tribulation will begin. No doubt the

chaos and confusion created by the disappearance of millions of people worldwide at the Rapture will make the environment ripe for the Antichrist to quickly rise to the top. The world will be desperate for answers. For solutions. For someone who can bring order.

Antichrist will catapult on the scene with answers, but the honeymoon won't last long because the world will soon be plunged into a terrible tribulation.

THE REMOVAL OF THE RESTRAINER

The apostle Paul continued in 2 Thessalonians 2 by tying the Rapture in with Antichrist in another way. He says that the Antichrist cannot be revealed until "he who now restrains" is taken out of the way. This restrainer is referred to both as a person and as a power.

> Let no one in any way deceive you, for it will not come unless the apostasy comes first, and the man of lawlessness is revealed, the son of destruction, who opposes and exalts himself

above every so-called god or object of worship, so that he takes his seat in the temple of God, displaying himself as being God. Do you not remember that while I was still with you, I was telling you these things? And you know what restrains him now, so that in his time he will be revealed. For the mystery of lawlessness is already at work; only he who now restrains will do so until he is taken out of the way. Then that lawless one will be revealed whom the Lord will slay with the breath of His mouth and bring to an end by the appearance of His coming. (2 Thessalonians 2:3–8)

God is telling us that one thing in particular is hindering the full outbreak of evil and opening of the door for Antichrist's entrance onto the world stage. And this hindrance can be called "the restrainer."

While there are many explanations of the identity of the restrainer, I believe the best view is that the restrainer is the Holy Spirit working in and through the church, the body of Christ on earth.[24]

There are four reasons for identifying "the

restrainer" as the restraining ministry of the Holy Spirit through the church.

1. This restraint requires omnipotent power. The only one with the power to restrain and hold back the appearance of Antichrist is God.

2. This is the only view that adequately explains the change in gender in 2 Thessalonians 2:6–7. The restrainer is both a power—"what restrains him now"—and a person—"he who now restrains." In Greek, the word *pneuma* (Spirit) is neuter. But the Holy Spirit is also consistently referred to by the masculine pronoun *He*, especially in John 14–16.

3. The Holy Spirit is spoken of in Scripture as restraining sin and evil in the world (see Genesis 6:3) and in the heart of the believer (see Galatians 5:16–17).

4. The church and its mission of proclaiming and portraying the gospel is the primary instrument the Holy Spirit uses in this age to restrain evil. We are the salt of the earth and the light of the world (see Matthew 5:13–16). We are

the temple of the Holy Spirit, both individually and corporately.

The restrainer, then, is the restraining influence and ministry of the Holy Spirit indwelling and working through His people in this present age.

I love the description of the identity of the restrainer by the famous Bible teacher Donald Grey Barnhouse.

> Well, what is keeping the Antichrist from putting in his appearance on the world stage? *You* are! You and every other member of the body of Christ on earth. The presence of the church of Jesus Christ is the restraining force that refuses to allow the man of lawlessness to be revealed. True, it is the Holy Spirit who is the real restrainer. But as both 1 Corinthians 3:16 and 6:19 teach, the Holy Spirit indwells the believer. The believer's body is the temple of the Spirit of God. Put all believers together then, with the Holy Spirit indwelling each of us, and you have a formidable restraining force.

For when the church is removed at the Rapture, the Holy Spirit goes with the church insofar as His restraining power is concerned. His work in this age of grace will be ended. Henceforth, during the Great Tribulation, the Holy Spirit will still be here on earth, of course—for how can you get rid of God?—but He will not be indwelling believers as He does now. Rather, he will revert to His Old Testament ministry of "coming upon" special people.[25]

When the Rapture occurs, the Spirit-indwelt church and its restraining influence will be removed. Satan will then be able to put his plan into full swing by bringing his man onto center stage to take control of the world. The Rapture will remove the one hindrance to the full outbreak of evil in the world through Antichrist and will throw the door wide open for him to come to power.

LOOKING FOR CHRIST

We must remember this important fact: The Antichrist will not be revealed until after the church is

taken to heaven. Until everyone who has personally trusted Jesus Christ as their Savior has seen our Lord face-to-face. Therefore, no one can know the identity of the Antichrist until we are raptured to heaven.

That's why believers are never told to look for Antichrist, but for Christ.

We are looking for the One whose name is above every name, before whom every knee shall bow and every tongue confess that He is Lord, to the glory of God the Father (see Philippians 2:9–11).

EIGHT

ANTICHRIST IS ALIVE AND WELL

I n her book, *My Life and Prophecies,* Jeanne Dixon recounted a vision she had at 7:00 a.m. on February 5, 1962, revealing that Antichrist had been born somewhere in the Middle East.

She believed he was possibly a descendant of Pharaoh Ikhnaton and Queen Nefertiti. Dixon also predicted that the Antichrist's power would continue to grow until 1999, when he would unveil his new religion.[26]

In 1982, a Mexican sect located at a site called New Jerusalem, 180 miles northwest of Mexico City, reported that the Antichrist was alive. Several members of the sect claimed to have Marian visions. One of the visionaries was a peasant girl named Mama

Maria de Jesus, who claimed to speak in the voice of the angel Gabriel. Her message was, "The Pope is a fraud Pope. Paul VI [who died in 1978] is imprisoned in the basement of the Vatican so that Antichrist can enter. The Antichrist is already here. He is 29 years old and comes from Guadalajara, and soon he will be called to Rome."[27]

These false prophets or prophetesses verify the fact that only the true God can tell the future accurately. But they do highlight the fact that many people are expecting the Antichrist to rise on the world scene.

With six chapters of background, we've finally made it to the big question: Is the Antichrist alive today? So what can we say about this question that so many are wondering about today. Is he, or isn't he?

EASY AS ONE, TWO, THREE

I believe there are at least three key parts to this answer. And it's important that we clearly grasp all three parts, so there is no misunderstanding.

First, I want to make it crystal clear that I don't believe anyone can say for sure that the Antichrist is alive today. As we observed in the last chapter, the

Antichrist will not be revealed until after believers have been raptured to glory. So you are wasting your time in trying to figure out if some particular person in Washington, London, Paris, or Rome is the Antichrist. According to the Scriptures, he will be revealed only when he makes his peace covenant with Israel. That will be his formal introduction to the world, and that takes place *after* God's people are in heaven.

Second, while no one knows if *the* Antichrist is alive today, we can be certain that *an* antichrist is alive in the world at this very moment. Writing late in the first century A.D., the apostle John said that the spirit of antichrist was already at work undermining and opposing the work of God (see 1 John 2:18; 4:3). The apostle Paul also said that, in his day, Satan was already at work, trying to bring Antichrist on the scene (see 2 Thessalonians 2:6–7). We can be certain that the *spirit* of antichrist is alive and well today!

I believe that Satan has a man ready in every generation, a Satanically prepared vessel to take center stage and rule the world. After all, this is Satan's goal (see Isaiah 14:12–14). God has stated that He will rule

the world through His Son, the Christ, so Satan's goal is to usurp God and rule the world through his man, the Antichrist. Since the devil doesn't know when the coming of Christ to establish His kingdom will occur, he is prepared in every generation with his man to try to take over the world and to stand against Christ and the establishment of his glorious kingdom.

We can see this by getting a quick overview of history.

- In the years after the flood, Satan ruled the world of that day through a mighty leader named Nimrod (see Genesis 10:8–12; 11:1–9).
- In the early days of Israel's history, Satan ruled a large part of the known world through Pharaoh.
- Later, in about 600 B.C., came the mighty Babylonian monarch Nebuchadnezzar (see Daniel 1–4).
- Then came possibly the greatest of them all— Alexander the Great (see Daniel 8:5–8, 21; 11:2–4).

- Satan persecuted Israel mercilessly through a Syrian king named Antiochus Epiphanes, in about 165 B.C.
- Satan made his greatest strides toward world domination through the Roman Caesars.
- He tried again with Napoleon.
- Then Hitler.
- Then Stalin.

And I firmly believe that Satan has someone picked out today, someone he can use to set up a rival kingdom to usurp the rightful place of the King of kings if the situation presents itself. There is always *an* Antichrist ready somewhere, prepared by Satan. I believe Satan has someone, somewhere, right now.

Third, while I want to reemphasize that I can't say for sure whether *the* Antichrist is alive today, I wouldn't be surprised if he is. All the key clues seem to be lining up.

Consider what we have seen.

Key Biblical Clues	The World Stage Today
Antichrist will rise from a ten-kingdom form of the reunited Roman Empire.	The European Union is now firmly in place. It does not yet exist in a ten-kingdom form as predicted in Scripture, but the goals of the EU parallel the Biblical predictions of an end-time power in Europe.
Antichrist will rise on a platform of peace for the Middle East.	The Middle East crisis is the number one international problem in the world today.
Antichrist will sit in the rebuilt temple in Jerusalem declaring that he is God.	Israel became a nation in May 1948 and seized control of Jerusalem in June 1967. And there is a movement today to rebuild the temple.
Antichrist will rule the entire enitire world politically, economically, and religiously.	Globalism, or globalization, is a present reality. In fact, given our current world climate it's a necessity.
Antichrist will force all people to take his mark of allegiance	The technology and acceptability of such a practice is gaining ground.

Just think about it. If Jesus is coming within the next forty to fifty years, then the Antichrist is almost certainly alive right now. While the Bible never tells us how old Antichrist will be when he comes on the world scene, we would assume he would be in his forties or fifties. Moreover, while I am certainly not saying that Jesus *is* coming in the next forty to fifty years, because no on can set a time for His coming, I do think is it highly probable. If this is true, then the Antichrist is alive somewhere on the earth today. He may even be on the world political scene waiting in the wings for his moment.

Again, all the clues seem to point in the same direction.

The emergence of Antichrist could be very soon. And that means the coming of the Lord is even closer.

Are you ready to meet Him?

NINE

DON'T IGNORE THE WARNING!

I'll never forget seeing the movie *The Omen* for the first time in 1976 when I was in high school. While the movie is a fictional horror film, its basic theme is sound—the Antichrist is coming, and he may even be alive and walking the earth right now. Its warning is very real. Antichrist is coming.

There is a gripping scene early in the movie. On the morning after the nightmarish fifth birthday party for Damien (the Antichrist), a Catholic priest named Father Brennan pays an unannounced visit to Ambassador Thorn's office. As soon as Father Brennan is alone with Thorn (Damien's father), he blurts out a startling warning to the ambassador: "You must accept Christ as your Savior. You must accept Him—now!"

Ambassador Thorn is stunned as the priest proceeds to tell him that his young son is really the son of Satan—the Antichrist. Thorn is incensed and calls for the security guards to haul the priest away. Father Brennan's warning to accept Christ is considered foolish by Thorn. Interestingly, however, even when Thorn finally realizes that Damien is the Antichrist, he still refuses to accept Christ.

ACCEPT CHRIST NOW!

The same warning is still applicable today. "Your must accept Christ as your Savior. You must accept Him—now!"

When the Antichrist appears, Scripture teaches that most people will still refuse to accept Christ and will instead turn from Him to follow the lawless one. Second Thessalonians 2:8–12 says,

> Then that lawless one will be revealed whom the Lord will slay with the breath of His mouth and bring to an end by the appearance of His coming; that is, the one whose coming is in accord with the activity of Satan, with all

power and signs and false wonders, and with all the deception of wickedness for those who perish, because they did not receive the love of the truth so as to be saved. For this reason God will send upon them a deluding influence so that they will believe what is false, in order that they all may be judged who did not believe the truth, but took pleasure in wickedness.

Don't count on waiting and receiving Christ later. No one knows when he or she might die, and one certainly doesn't know when the Rapture will occur.

Don't put it off any longer. Accept Jesus Christ as your Savior now!

The Bible tells us that when Jesus Christ died on the cross, He purchased a full pardon from the penalty of sin for you and me. The pardon has been bought and paid for, and God offers it to every person. All that we have to do to make this pardon effective in our lives is simply to receive it, to accept it.

Just take the offer and say, "Thank you."

"Not Unless You Take It!"

Years ago I heard a story about Dr. Walter Wilson of Kansas City. Dr. Wilson, who was a medical doctor and evangelist, was preaching at a church on the final night of a weeklong series of meetings. Dr. Wilson was trying his best to make the message of the gospel crystal clear, so anyone there could understand God's plan of salvation.

At the end of the meeting, Dr. Wilson used a great illustration for a doctor. He said, "Let's pretend you are very sick, and the only thing that will cure your illness is this medicine here that I prescribe for you. Now, let me ask you a question. Will the medicine do you any good?"

There was a prolonged time of uncomfortable silence in the church auditorium. Finally, a young boy in the back couldn't stand it any longer and hollered out, "Not unless you take it!"

Dr. Wilson's face lit up. He said, "That's exactly right. It won't do you a bit of good unless you take it."

I realize that this story is very simple, but if you have never accepted Christ you need to take the gift of eternal life right now. If you have never accepted

Christ as your Savior, then you have a very serious problem—a sin problem. It's fatal, deadly, and eternal in its consequences. But God has just the remedy for the problem. Jesus paid it all. He died for your sins on the cross and rose again from the dead as proof that God accepted in full the payment that He made.

Now all you have to do is receive it. John 1:12 says, "But to all who believed him and accepted him, he gave the right to become the children of God" (NLT).

CALL UPON THE NAME
OF THE LORD

God promises in His Word that "WHOEVER WILL CALL ON THE NAME OF THE LORD WILL BE SAVED" (Romans 10:13). Why not call on Him in faith right now, accepting Christ and his gifts of forgiveness of sin and eternal life. There are no magic words that you have to say, but you might want to call upon the Lord by repeating this simple prayer:

> *Lord, I admit that I am a sinner. I have gone my own way in life and have broken Your laws and*

commands. I recognize that I cannot save myself by my own good works. I must have a Savior. And I believe that Jesus Christ is the Savior who died for me on the cross and rose again. I receive Him now by faith, trusting in Him alone for salvation from sin. Thank You for the free gift of salvation through Christ. Amen.

If you have prayed this prayer, let someone know. Find a Bible-teaching, loving church to attend. And find a way to serve the Lord who gave Himself for you.

His coming may be very soon. May He find us faithful, ready, and expectant when He comes.

FAMOUS LAST WORDS

Last words are always important. They often tell us a great deal about a person. People often save their most important instructions, profound thoughts, deepest concerns, and heartfelt expressions for last. Have you ever thought about the last words of Jesus? We find them in the final chapter of the Bible—Revelation 22.

"Behold, I am coming quickly, and My reward is with Me, to render to every man according to what he

has done. I am the Alpha and the Omega, the first and the last, the beginning and the end" (Revelation 22:12–13).

"Yes, I am coming quickly" (Revelation 22:20).

The only proper response to these last words is "Amen. Come, Lord Jesus!"

I hope you're ready!

The publisher and author would love to hear your comments about this book. *Please contact us at:* www.multnomah.net/hitchcock

APPENDIX

THE TOP TEN KEYS TO ANTICHRIST'S IDENTITY

1. He will not be recognized until after the rapture of believers to heaven.

2. He will begin insignificantly and will then rise to world prominence as a man of peace.

3. He will be a Gentile world leader from Europe.

4. He will rule over the reunited Roman Empire (the unholy Roman Empire).

5. He will make a seven-year peace covenant with Israel.

6. He will be assassinated and will come back to life.

7. He will break his treaty with Israel at the midpoint of the Tribulation and will invade the land.

8. He will sit in the temple of God and will declare himself to be God.

9. He will desecrate the temple in Jerusalem by having an image of himself placed in it.

10. He will rule the world politically, economically, and religiously for three and a half years.

Twenty-Five Things You Need to Know About the Antichrist and the End Times

1. He will appear in "the time of the end" of Israel's history (see Daniel 8:17).

2. His manifestation will signal the beginning of the Day of the Lord (see 2 Thessalonians 2:1–3).

3. His manifestation is currently being hindered by "the restrainer" (see 2 Thessalonians 2:3–7).

4. His rise to power will come through peace programs (see Revelation 6:2). He will make a covenant of peace with Israel (see Daniel 9:27). This event will signal the beginning of the seven-year tribulation. He will later break that covenant at its midpoint.

5. Near the middle of the Tribulation, he will be assassinated or violently killed (see Daniel 11:45; Revelation 13:3, 12, 14).

6. He will descend into the abyss (see Revelation 17:8).

7. He will be raised back to life (see Revelation 11:7; 13:3, 12, 14; 17:8).

8. The whole world will be amazed and will follow after

him (see Revelation 13:3).

9. He will be totally controlled and energized by Satan (see Revelation 13:2–5).

10. He will subdue three of the ten kings in the reunited Roman Empire (see Daniel 7:24).

11. The kings will give all authority to the Beast (see Revelation 17:12–13).

12. He will invade the land of Israel and desecrate the rebuilt temple (see Daniel 9:27; 11:41; 12:11; Matthew 24:15; Revelation 11:2).

13. He will mercilessly pursue and persecute the Jewish people (see Daniel 7:21, 25; Revelation 12:4–6).

14. He will set himself up in the temple as God and be worshiped for three and a half years (see 2 Thessalonians 2:4; Revelation 13:4–8).

15. His claim to deity will be accompanied by great signs and wonders (see 2 Thessalonians 2:9–12).

16. He will speak great blasphemies against God (see Daniel 7:8; Revelation 13:6).

17. He will rule the world politically, religiously and economically for three and a half years (see Revelation 13:4–8, 16–18).

18. He will be promoted by a second beast who will lead the world in worship of him (see Revelation 13:11–18).

19. He will require all to receive his mark (666) to buy and sell (see Revelation 13:16–18).

20. He will establish his political and economic capital in Babylon (see Revelation 17).

21. He and the ten kings will destroy Babylon (see Revelation 18:16).

22. He will kill the two witnesses (see Revelation 11:7).

23. He will gather all the nations against Jerusalem (see Zechariah 12:1–2; 14:1–3; Revelation 16:16; 19:19).

24. He will fight against Christ when He returns to earth and will suffer total defeat (see Revelation 19:19).

25. He will be cast alive into the lake of fire (see Daniel 7:11; Revelation 19:20).

NOTES

1.   Jeffery L. Sheler and Mike Tharp, "Dark Prophecies," *U.S. News and World Report,* 15 December 1997, n.p.

2.   Billy Graham, "My Answer," *The Daily Oklahoman,* 12 April 2002.

3.   Kenneth L. Woodward, "What the Bible Says about the End of the World," *Newsweek,* 1 November 1999, 69.

4.   Arthur W. Pink, *The Antichrist* (Grand Rapids, Mich.: Kregel Publications, 1988), 9.

5.   Grant R. Jeffrey, *Prince of Darkness* (Toronto: Frontier Research Publications, 1994), 29.

6.   Ibid., 30.

7.   J. Dwight Pentecost, *Will Man Survive?* (Grand Rapids, Mich.: Zondervan Publishing House, 1971), 93.

8.   "Europe Wakes Up to New Year and New Currency" *CNN,* 1 January 1999. htttp://www.cnn.com/WORLD/europe/9812/31/euro.01/ (accessed August 12, 2002).

9.   The use of the word *firm (gabar)* could simply mean that the covenant will be made strong, sure, or certain. (Leon Wood, *A Commentary on Daniel* [Grand Rapids, Mich.: Zondervan Publishing House, 1973], 258.) But I prefer the idea suggested by Walvoord that the treaty will be an imposed, compelled, and forced accord. (John F. Walvoord, *Major Bible Prophecies: 37 Crucial Prophecies That Affect You Today* [Grand Rapids, Mich.: Zondervan Publishing House, 1993], 319.)

10.   Walvoord, *Major Bible Prophecies,* 319.

11.   There are three other main views on the identity of the rider on the white horse in Revelation 6:1–2: (1) Jesus Christ, (2) the spirit of militarism and conquest, and (3) the gospel of Christ. However, I believe that the best view is to see this rider as a movement of false messiahs who will come on the scene after the Rapture, of which the Antichrist will be the prime example. The main support for this view is the striking similarity between Matthew 24 and Revelation 6. Both accounts follow the same sequence:

	Matthew 24	*Revelation 6*
Deception by antichrists	verses 4–5	verses 1–2
War	verses 6–7	verses 3–4
Famine	verse 7	verses 5–6
Death	verses 7–9	verses 7–8
Martyrdom	verses 9–10	verses 9–11
Cosmological disturbances	verse 29	verses 12–17

For a more thorough discussion of this issue, see Daniel K. K. Wong, "The First Horseman of Revelation 6," *Bibliotheca Sacra* 153 (April–June 1996): 212–26.

12.   Arnold Fruchtenbaum, *The Footsteps of the Messiah* (Tustin, Calif.: Ariel Ministries, 1983), 174.

13.   Daniel 12:11 says that the abomination of desolation will stand in the holy place for 1,290 days. That's the final three and a half years of the Tribulation (1,260 days) plus thirty extra days. Why an extra thirty days? When Jesus returns at His second coming at the end of the Tribulation, Antichrist will be destroyed, but evidently the image will remain in the temple for another thirty days beyond that time, and then it, too, will be removed and destroyed.

14.   Here are three of the more common solutions to this problem:

1.   Some believe that the temple could be rebuilt without disturbing the Dome of the Rock. The Jewish temple and Muslim Dome of the Rock could stand side by side on the Temple Mount. This is very unlikely for two reasons. First, the best archaeologists, including Israeli scholars, concur that the Dome of the Rock stands on the site where the first and second Jewish temples once stood. Second, even if the temple could be rebuilt next to the Dome of the Rock, this would be anathema to both the Jews and the Muslims. Neither of them would accept this solution.

2.   It is also possible that God will send some great disaster, such as an earthquake, that will destroy the Muslim structures on the Temple Mount.

3.   A third possible solution is that the annihilation of Russia and her Muslim allies, as detailed in Ezekiel 38–39, will eliminate the Muslim threat to the Jews, thus allowing them to tear down the Dome of the Rock and Al-Aqsa Mosque and rebuild their temple without fear of reprisal.

15.   Randall Price, *The Coming Last Days Temple* (Eugene, Ore.: Harvest House Publishers, 1999), 592.

16.   Fruchtenbaum, *The Footsteps of the Messiah,* 173.

17.   Ibid.

18.   John F. Walvoord, *The Prophecy Knowledge Handbook* (Wheaton, Ill.: SP Publications, 1990), 587.

19. M. R. DeHaan, *Studies in Revelation* (Grand Rapids, Mich.: Zondervan, 1946; reprint, Grand Rapids, Mich.: Kregel Publications, 1998), 189.

20. Henry Morris, *The Revelation Record* (Wheaton, Ill.: Tyndale House Publishers, 1983), 256.

21. Ibid., 252.

22. John F. Walvoord, *Prophecy: Fourteen Essential Keys to Understanding the Final Drama* (Nashville: Thomas Nelson Publishers, 1993), 125.

23. Steven Levy, "Playing the ID Card," *Newsweek,* 13 May 2002, 44–6.

24. There are at lest eleven different views on the identity of the restrainer in 2 Thessalonians 2: (1) the Roman Empire, (2) the Jewish state, (3) the apostle Paul, (4) the preaching of the gospel, (5) human government, (6) Satan, (7) Elijah, (8) some unknown heavenly being, (9) Michael the archangel, (10) the Holy Spirit, and (11) the church

25. Donald Grey Barnhouse, ed., *Thessalonians: An Expositional Commentary* (Grand Rapids, Mich.: Zondervan Publishing House, 1977), 99–100.

26. Jeanne Dixon, *My Life and Prophecies,* 179–80, as cited by H. L. Wilmington, *The King Is Coming* (Wheaton, Ill.: Tyndale House Publishers, 1973), 89–91.

27. *New York Times,* 12 November 1982, as cited by Bernard McGinn, *Antichrist: Two Thousand Years of the Human Fascination with Evil* (San Francisco: Harper, 1994), 251.

"The End Is Near!"

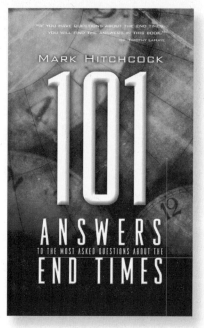

"If you have questions about the end times you, will find the answers in this book."

—DR. TIMOTHY LAHAYE

The end is near! Or is it? The Antichrist is alive and well today! *Or is he?* The church is about to be raptured and will certainly escape the Tribulation…*right?* When it comes to the end times, there's so much confusion. Preachers with elaborate charts share their theories about Revelation and other prophetic books of the Bible. "Ah, Babylon stands for the United States," they say. But then other teachers share their theories: "No, Babylon stands for the Roman Catholic Church, or the European Union, or the literal Babylon rebuilt in Iraq…." *Would somebody please shoot straight with me?* Finally, someone has. Gifted scholar and pastor Mark Hitchcock walks you gently through Bible prophecy in an engaging, user-friendly style. Hitchcock's careful examination of the topic will leave you feeling informed and balanced in your understanding of events to come…in our time?

ISBN 1-57673-952-X

Hitchcock Examines Bible Prophecy's Silence About America

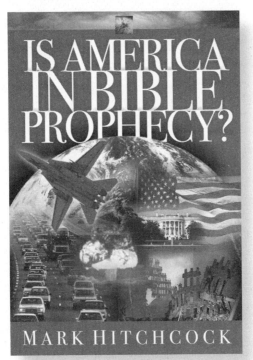

In *Is America in Bible Prophecy?*, expert Mark Hitchcock deals with often-raised questions about America's future. Examining three prophetic passages that are commonly thought to describe America, Hitchcock concludes that the Bible is actually silent about the role of the United States in the end times. He then discusses the implications of America's absence in prophetic writings. Along with Hitchcock's compelling forecast for the future, he offers specific actions Americans can take to keep their nation strong and blessed by God, as well as an appendix of additional questions and answers.

ISBN 1-57673-496-X

What's Your Biggest Worry About the End Times?

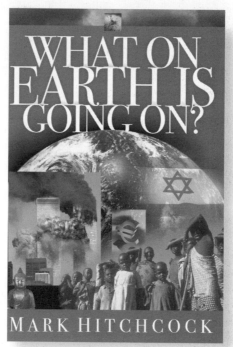

As sensationalists and skeptics wreak havoc with the country's emotions, prophecy expert Mark Hitchcock provides a much-needed definition of what is meant by signs of the times. In *What on Earth Is Going On?*, Hitchcock discusses the current interest in prophecy caused by the 9/11 attack, presents Jesus' own forecast for the future of the world, and details five major global developments today that discernibly signal Christ's coming. This balanced, concise overview of the real signs of the times will clarify Christ's instructions challenging His followers to be alert in the final days. Readers will easily find and absorb the information they need to prepare for His return.

ISBN 1-57673-853-1

Get Ready for the Invasion...

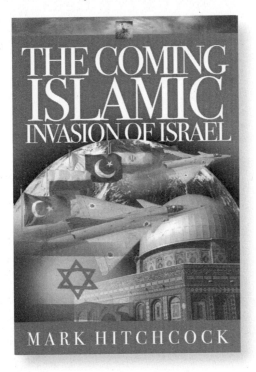

Writing 2,500 years ago, the prophet Ezekiel predicted a Russian-Islamic invasion of Israel in the last days. The third book in Mark Hitchcock's fascinating prophecy series explains the relevance of this prediction to today's world. First, he establishes how the current global scene sets the stage for this event and focuses on the identity of the invading nations (those mentioned in Ezekiel are like a *Who's Who* of Israel's current enemies). Hitchcock then considers the time and motives for their attack. Finally, he discusses God's dramatic intervention that will pave the way for the Antichrist's worldwide empire.

ISBN 1-59052-048-3